COMING TO CHRIST

COMING TO CHRIST

And So You Will Bear Testimony To Me

CORTEZ PERRY

PALMETTO
PUBLISHING
Charleston, SC
www.PalmettoPublishing.com

Copyright © 2024 by Cortez Perry

All rights reserved

No portion of this book may be reproduced, stored in a retrieval system, or transmitted in any form by any means—electronic, mechanical, photocopy, recording, or other—except for brief quotations in printed reviews, without prior permission of the author.

Paperback ISBN: 979-8-8229-3831-1
eBook ISBN: 979-8-8229-3832-8

PREFACE

While I was praying in my room one afternoon during the first week in April 2018, the Holy Spirit said to me, "Make a book named *Coming to Christ* about stories of different people and how they came to the Lord God." I opened my eyes and wrote down on my nightstand what was told to me and the people and stories to include in the book. "These are the stories" Forward by Holy Spirit.

TABLE OF CONTENTS

1. Greasy Row   1
2. Child, "Please!!!"   15
3. The Spirit Is Able   21
4. You Just Don't Know   35
5. Bulldog "Warrior"   53
6. Let Me Do Me!   69
7. Righteous   87
8. Somebody Help Me   105

Chapter One

GREASY ROW

But God chose the foolish things of the world to shame the wise; God chose the weak things of the world to shame the strong.

1 Corinthians 1:27

In Belzoni, Mississippi, also known as "Greasy Row," right off Highway 49W in the delta region of the Yazoo River, a child of exceptional intelligence was born. Many in his time may not have thought so because of a hindering speech impediment: a stutter. He was born to parents who were passing time together, more acquaintances than anything else.

His father left and headed north shortly after his birth, having another child with his long-term girlfriend due three months later (who would receive his surname Jr.) in search of new land and opportunity. His mother soon married Mr. Robert, who took to the child like he was his own.

Growing up, he went to school in Mississippi and lived with his mom and Mr. Robert and stayed up north with his father, his father's wife, and his brother Jr. in the summers. He would get all his school clothes (slick and cool) and occasionally some of Jrs. clothes from the city. Then he'd head home and style on the other country boys.

Somewhere along the line in his teen years, he developed a thrill-seeking, daredevil personality, a taste for adrenaline, the need for speed. Maybe in part to distract from his stutter, he would do crazy things to stop folks from focusing on that. Or maybe it was to show the others that he was down to earth and not Highfalutin, like some thought, even though he was smart and they were well off. (Mr. Robert was a business owner, one of the only Blacks in Belzoni.) Or maybe it was because he spent a good deal of time up north in the big bad city and wanted to show out for the crowds.

On any account, he would wheelie his bicycle for blocks at the time. Or take his motorcycle and ride with his feet up on the handlebars. Or stand up on the seat for people to marvel at him, jump ditches with his car—you name it, anything for the rush.

Time came for college. He finished high school with honors and decided to attend Mississippi State University in Starkville, Mississippi. This school was infamous for its long history of bigotry and hatred to Blacks. In addition, he decided to sell ready-rock base cocaine (crack) while he attended MSU. He didn't need to sell drugs to pay for his tuition. He didn't need it for his lodging or meal plan. He didn't need it to help out with the family back home because they were having financial difficulty. No! He came to college and sold drugs for the thrill of it. For the rush and the arrogant thought of having superior mind power and the ability to outsmart any small-town laws. After all, he spent his summers "up north."

Junior year, first semester, he was in his off-campus apartment getting ready for class when the Starkville police department came knocking. They took him to the station while they searched every piece of the apartment. They didn't find any evidence, because a few weeks prior to this bust, he got a tip from an SPD officer, who was a customer, that he was a target and they would be coming. So, he moved everything to another place he had across town. Being well versed in the drug laws and confident in his operation, he had no fear of being caught with anything, let alone going to jail for it.

After all, he was in college with a double major in biomedical engineering and abstract architecture. He was outperforming any of the whites in those majors, and he was from a well-to-do, prominent family in their area, plus he'd never been in any type of trouble and had absolutely no record whatsoever.

What he didn't count on was the deep-seated hatred for Blacks in Mississippi. He was charged with the distribution of narcotics and sentenced to sixty-five years in the Mississippi prison system on three counts alone while awaiting sentencing for twelve other miscellaneous infractions. The family posted three different bails of $20,000, $15,000, and $50,000, and Mr. Robert sold his long-standing business for him to be released. When all was said and done, the sentence stuck! He was sent to Parchman, one of the most violent, dangerous penitentiaries in the entire South. He was one year and a semester away from completing his college degree with a double major, no less. The family stuck by his side through two unsuccessful appeals: three years, over $100,000 in attorney fees, plus the strain and toll of dishonor to their family name.

While in prison, the young man decided to pick up the Bible (King James) and read it. A change happened in his mind, body, and spirit. He stopped searching for ways to avoid his sentence. He drew near to God to the point of attending prison Bible study for the morning, afternoon, and evening sessions. He eventually began leading those sessions.

The time came for the third and final appeal. The family was fully behind him, 100 percent, as usual, only at this point they were under financial strain due to lawyer fees and Mr. Robert selling his business. The only means they had was to place their home up as collateral for the cost. They did so and made no mention of it to him at all.

The attorney came to visit and let out that the family was using their home as collateral, and he was devastated. He thought about how there was no way he could let them lose the house because of the decisions he'd made. They had given him a proper upbringing, a good home, a great name, and an example to live up to. He didn't have to do any of the things he did.

That day, he fired the attorney. The same night, he came to God with fear and thanksgiving and said, "Lord, I know all things—anything—is possible through you. Please let your will be done in my life. I've tried every way I know to get out of this. I've put my family through enough; I only want to go with you, Lord. Let your will be done, not my own. And if you see fit for me to do all these sixty-five years, so be it. I believe you will never leave nor forsake me."

He went through his final appeal with no lawyer, no shield, and no excuses, just the Lord God. The prior weekend, the missionary who came in and conducted the prison ministry, attended a $1500-a-plate event. He spoke to his masonic brothers about this young man at the prison and how he had grown in

God and the ministry. One of the brothers he spoke with at the dinner was a member of the parole board and appeal committee. That following Tuesday, his appeal was granted and he was released shortly after. The state never prosecuted him for the twelve pending charges that were left.

Even though he didn't get caught with anything, he was guilty of violating God's universal law and all the gifts and advantages afforded him. He knew that all of this happened to draw him to the Most High God. He is now a minister and has served the good Lord for over thirty years since that night in his cell. God is the greatest!

Chapter Two

CHILD, "PLEASE!!!"

Jesus said, "Let the little children come to me, and do not hinder them, for the kingdom of heaven belongs to such as these."

Matthew 19:14

This story is a great testimony as we meet a six-year-old girl living with a drug-addicted mom and a homosexual dad. Her father is very nice, and she loves him, but he lives in another city some hours away. She's stuck with her crack-smoking mother who often leaves her at school or at the neighbor's house for weeks at a time. Occasionally, her dad, who had contracted AIDS, gets her for holidays and some summers. So, he is unable to know what is happening on a day-to-day basis. And this would never have happened if he'd had any knowledge of it.

One day, when she was about eight, she was sent to her room while her mom had company. This happened often because that's when they'd get high. She sat down on the floor in her room playing with toys, and suddenly, she could feel God's presence, like a big hug wrapping around her, very calming, peaceful, and safe. She felt protected, as if He'd said, "Nothing can affect or harm you."

After that, she would sit on their porch and a church van began coming around twice a week. On Wednesdays it would take her to Bible study—or kids church, as she knew it—and on Sundays, it would take her to service. Now, her mom never objected, or her mom didn't even recognize she was gone from the porch, and this allowed her to learn who God is.

Growing in God, she got to the point where her mom began attending church with her, and her mom got herself off drugs. Then the pastor made a pass at her mother and set her back. She relapsed, but by then they both had already come to Christ. Soon after joining another church, they brought their family members, some of whom were on drugs themselves, and friends who were users, and they came to Christ. Eventually, they both became ministers and members of the clergy. All this came from the little girl being able to recognize the presence of God when she needed Him most. Amen.

Chapter Three

THE SPIRIT IS ABLE

Watch and pray so that you will not fall into temptation. The spirit is willing, but the flesh is weak.

Matthew 26:41

A young man resides in Madison, Wisconsin, with his mom. He never knew who his father was. In fact, this teen has just recently become the father of his own child, a precious little girl. This jewel wasn't a plan of his, and he and the mother weren't greatly in love with one another but were more or less good friends. He's grown up in a single-parent household, and he wants more for his daughter. He decides he should educate himself. By doing so, he can provide a better life for her.

He goes to Howard University, a prestigious HBCU located in Washington DC, nicknamed "Chocolate City" after all the beautiful black people there. This young man is away from home for the first time and is into the same things as most other young adults entering college: parties, girls, smoking, and gangster rap (in the NWA, Ice Cube, Tupac era). He gets tight with a guy from Compton, California, and they soon bond over similar tastes in music, girls, and just college life in general. They are drinking buddies; on Friday nights they hang out, try to find a party, and do some girl hunting.

There is one particular girl the young man always seems to bring up to his friend while they rap. She isn't from the party scene like them and most of their other collegians, which is part of the appeal. She is cool, down to earth, attractive, but different. It is something about her. They become friends; he hopes of becoming more, she hopes to save his soul. See, what is so different about her is that she is a Christian and she takes her faith very seriously. He has never seen a person, not to mention a young person, who is so matter of fact and sure of herself the way she is. After all, he wasn't raised in church, by any means. His mother's parents, his grandparents, took him sometimes when he visited Milwaukee, but God? No way. He thought that was only for fanatics or people who were mentally lazy sheep, but she was none of those things.

If anyone has gone through the black college/HBCU experience, then you know that the administration isn't always the most organized or proficient. Parents and families of students would send care packages to students with money, food, clothes, supplies, etc. However, none of their packages were making it to the students for weeks at the time because of the dysfunction of the school. This led to a lot of students on campus being hungry. After the cafeteria closed at 7:00 p.m., it was a long time until 7:00 a.m. when it opened again for breakfast.

One night, the young man's stomach rumbles. He has no money (no care package in over a month), and it feels as if his stomach is touching his back, he's so hungry. He goes to the young lady's dorm just to see her and complain about still not receiving any mail. She allows him entrance and entertains his complaints, laughing at him while getting ready for her ICF meeting. She is meeting with other students for InterVarsity Christian Fellowship, a group of young Christians who are strong in the faith like her. During his protest, he mentions to her how he is starving and doesn't know what to do with himself. They finish talking, and as they are about to leave, she walks over to her cabinet, grabs a can of Campbell's soup, and places it in his hand while they stand there at the door.

He says, "When I saw you grab the soup from the cabinet, I also saw it was the only thing in the cabinet at all. Why would you give me the only thing you have, the very last thing you have for yourself to eat?"

She stares at him in the doorway and says simply, "Because that's what I'm supposed to do."

When he returns to his room, he eats the soup. Then he turns the music off and lays down, but he can't wrap his mind around what she did and said to him. He turns out the bed, kneels, having never prayed or bent his knee before. He comes to God and prays, "To the God of my girlfriend and of intervarsity Christian Fellowship, if you are the one true and living God, show yourself. Prove to me you exist; let me know you are real, and I will follow and serve you from this day forward."

He climbs back into bed, closes his eyes for twenty minutes or so, and is awakened by a knock at the door. He jumps up and opens the door, and there stands a man he has never seen before. The guy proceeds to explain he's also a student and he lives on the tenth floor of the adjacent building. The visitor says while he was lying in bed, the Spirit told him, "Go down to the fourth floor of this building and minister to the person in the room where I send you."

He invites the guy in and they begin to talk about what had just happen to them both, God's love, and hope for mankind.

The stranger prays with him and asks, "Are you ready to give your life to the Lord?"

The young man looks intensely back at him and answers, "No!" He totally backs out of the promise he just made to God, even after all he had just witnessed.

His drinking buddy comes by the next day (who turned out to be an Oscar-nominated, Emmy-winning actor) for the usual drinking, smoking, and listening to their music. The only thing is, the Spirit had changed the young man. He couldn't enjoy their normal activities now. He tells his buddy Anthony what happened to him the night before and introduces him to the girl, who later becomes Anthony's wife. The young man takes down all his posters, won't drink, won't smoke, and stops listening to the violent and vulgar music he loved so much.

After a week or so passed, he is ready. He goes to an ICF prayer meeting, and the guy from the tenth floor who had come to his room is leading the prayer. Right then, at that moment he confesses that Jesus died and was raised on the third day and He sits at the right hand of the Father. Saved!

The young man does not finish school at Howard. He goes back home the following semester, and after a year, at age twenty-one, he starts a church. It begins with five members and grows to one hundred inside of three years. Today, he is a pastor in a major metropolitan city of a church with well over five hundred members. God is the greatest.

Chapter Four

YOU JUST DON'T KNOW

If any of you lacks wisdom, you should ask God, who gives generously to all without finding fault, and it will be given to you.

James 1:5

I entered my freshman year at Lane College in January 2001—the same year of the 9/11 attacks on the U.S. I started college at the age of twenty because I never thought I would live past eighteen. I grew up in the country, raised in a gambling house. I witnessed the lies, lust, and greed for power of so-called people of respect: community leaders, business owners, and influential persons of the area who made policy, etc. Then I came to the city with no brothers, large family, or notorious name to protect me. I learned quickly that the most violent person gets the best response and respect. I survived when friends or people I knew were murdered. I myself had been shot and had shot others. It was just the way it was. I knew that every day I may have to kill or be killed. Another reason I was certain I wouldn't make it out of my teens was because of a dream I'd had in which I saw my tombstone with a date of 1998, the year of my eighteenth birthday. Because of these compelling reasons, I wholeheartedly expected my expiration at a young age.

By the time I thought to take inventory of my life, I looked up and was twenty. I had gotten my diploma from an alternative school (not the school I attended for four years and was so proud to be a part of because I'd helped to build the school's and my infamous reputation.) I had a two-year-old old son. My name was solidified in the city. I had a distaste for street life. And I had the realization that I had absolutely *no clue* what to do at this stage in life. Because I'd never planned to see it.

In the summer of 2000, I was driving in the ghetto, contemplating my newfound reality, when I noticed a classmate from school (the four-year that helped make my name, that I loved, that didn't let me walk across the stage. Not the alternative school where I took night classes and was salutatorian because I figured out how to manipulate the computer testing system they used to evaluate comprehension). The truth is, I never paid much attention to this girl while we were together in school at all and considered myself out of her league. I was a hot boy and normally liked fast girls, but when I saw her running headed into a church, that sparked my interest.

We exchanged numbers and grew close over the summer. She went back to school; I went back to the street. Then we began dating long-distance. We used a lot of phone cards and two-way paging. This was before free nights and weekends or texting. She was deep; I respected her perspective and her faith.

Coming from the South, I always knew of God, but I wasn't raised in church and didn't have to attend, unlike most Southerners, so I didn't know the principles of God. I'd had a cousin named Shell from my dad's side who came and got me from my grandma's great grand house. This was really something because it was considered an unholy place in our area due to the type of activity and services we provided. However, she came and took me to church once or twice. I knew it was important because they let me go with her without any friction. She would pull up at the end of the road—a really long driveway—and drop me off the same way.

The closer I got to this young lady, the closer I drew to God. I could see firsthand how her faith was a factor in every part of her life, and that astonished me. She was back in school for the semester. And I was in the city with a child I never planned to have. The child's mother and I never dated; she was a fast girl and one of many I was only having sex with recklessly. We were paired with one another simply because of our status. I had no means to provide for my son because I'd vowed to God never to sell drugs again after getting out of a life-altering incident. Plus, I learned my name would be included in a local and federal criminal indictment, along with some of my associates. Wiretap, jewelry, hotel car receipts, traffic camera photos out of state, the whole nine yards. *Done!*

She suggested I come to college where she was, get away, and change my scenery and view. I applied to the college and was denied. Having never seen the campus and knowing only one person in the entire state of Tennessee,

I packed two bags of clothes, $150 in pocket, and went anyway. I spoke to the president of the college, Dr Wesley Cornelius McClure, God bless his soul, and explained to him how I would be an asset and not a liability to the school. Also, I explained how he would be giving me a chance at a real life. After he finished watching the Tupac video playing in his office and that conversation, I was in!

The combination of dodging this indictment, the pressure of having a son whom I didn't want to go through what I had been through, and the love of this woman got me to this school. Once I got there, I could see and feel God working in my life to keep me there. I saw His hand in the relationships that I formed and in my living being provided for. I saw His hand when I wanted to come home and my coconspirator told me there was nothing for me back home and to stay at school. Then another coconspirator was murdered a month after I went away to school. We had just shared a room on the out-of-town trip that got us all indicted. I even saw His hand in not having any home to come back to in the city while away at school because my mom was in between homes.

I made it through my first semester, came back to the city, and was sleeping on my uncle's floor because there was no place for me to stay. I started going to church with my girlfriend and her family to Blessed Deliverance, which was held inside Carlton Street Elementary School. I attended nearly every Sunday that summer and grew in understanding. I began reading and developing a relationship with Jesus Christ for myself. I would mostly read the red words of the Bible, indicating when Jesus was speaking. In Matthew 6, I read how Jesus spoke of giving to the needy and not letting your left hand know what your right hand was doing. This stood out to me because I grew up hearing this term at home in the country pertaining to side deals between one another. Finding out these were God's words and what he truly meant them for blew me back. I learned that if a person gives, they should do it out of a loving heart, not for the credit or recognition of others.

I was not a member of the church I was attending. Before each service, they would set up folding chairs in rows in the gymnasium of the school, but they hoped to build a church of their own soon. When it came time for tithes and offerings, all the money I had to my name was maybe six dollars, if that. There I was, at twenty-one years of age, with five or six after having made thousands of dollars. I'd become accustomed to having that type of money from hustling since the fifth grade. It was sobering and humbling to find myself, at twenty-one, homeless and broke, to say the least.

I placed all of the money I had in the offering with the honest thought, "Maybe this will help the church in some small way, because the Lord can do more with it than I can." Pastor Anthony D. Lester went through the service. At the end, he asked the congregation of less than forty people for anyone preparing to return to school to come up in front to the altar. I wasn't a child, so I didn't move. He asked again, but I wasn't a member, so I still didn't move. He asked one last time (there were nine or ten people up there already) for whoever was going back to school, looked in my direction, and waved me up. I finally came and he handed me an envelope with a fifty-dollar bill in it! At that place in my life after all I had been through, for God to share His word with me, reveal Himself, and prove his word in front of me, I was amazed. He took what I gave out of true love and faith and increased it tenfold before I could leave the building. This was how I came to God!

How did it feel to learn that God is real? That Jesus is the way the truth and the light?

It felt like I hit the lottery of truth. Because of everything I had ever seen, I had wondered why Black people were treated like trash, both by others and by one another. I had wondered why so many of us were poor. I had wondered how I'd had so much money before, but I couldn't keep it, and I couldn't even explain where it went. I had wondered why there were very few people in my life whom I respected, and why even those few would let me down.

And then *it all made sense*.

It felt like people or forces had intentionally, purposely hidden this truth, this revelation, and this love from me my entire life.

It felt like I found myself. In that moment, God's love made everything clear and in order.

I felt grateful, hopeful, amazed, humbled, very thankful, and remorseful, not so much for my behavior, but for my thinking and mindset.

I felt like my life was saved in that moment. I had the OK to live a good life. I felt like someone had seen what had happened to me and that all the things I'd seen were not normal and it shouldn't have been the way it was when I grew up.

It felt indescribable, like scales had fallen from my eyes and I could finally see truly and clearly.

Thank you, Lord!

Chapter Five

BULLDOG "WARRIOR"

Truly I tell you, if you have faith as small as a mustard seed, you can say to this mountain, "Move from here to there; and it will move. Nothing will be impossible for you."

Matthew 17:20

Hey, my name is Chubbs. I'm from the west side of Chicago. I was born the lead dog of thirteen to a one-of-a-kind mom. I am a former pimp, hustler, and drug abuser, and this is how I came to God.

I find myself in Milwaukee, Wisconsin, living in the ghetto. I'm on leave from my neighborhood out west because of some things I've done and some I was protecting myself from doing. My preferred drug is ready rock "base" cocaine, also known as crack—stemming from a habit and era in the 70s when powder cocaine was an elitist recreational drug used as a matter of status and influence and deemed a "rich man's high" due to how expensive it was (two hundred dollars or more a gram in those days). This turned into a nasty crack indulgence once my brother was murdered and the older hustlers, I looked up to took interest in me. They were cool and did it, so I tried it also.

Now, before I was hooked, I was always the life of the party. I was very easygoing, and people loved being around me—I would make you feel like you owned the world. But when I used, that all changed. It made me aggressive and I had little to no patience.

At this moment, I'm three months behind on my rent. I have a full-time job, but all my money goes to support my habit. I go to the bank and pull all the money from my account. Then I head straight for any place I can pass a bad check. My landlord is calling me and leaving threatening voicemails because I won't answer. I've clearly chosen drugs over my relationships back home.

I don't get along with people at work. There are two guys who give me hell—well we give each other hell; I can give it as much as I get. This drug rules above every function of my life.

One night, I go outside. I walk around thinking about how to get high because I'm out of money. I owe my dope man for some credit he gave me, so I'm dodging him.

A woman I've never seen before says to me "What are you doing out here? You don't belong, you're not made for this out here."

This strikes a nerve in me because, being small and always having to prove myself in the neighborhood and among my family growing up, I want to prove to this woman I don't even know and to myself that I do belong in the streets and am tough.

I reply, "I'm a bulldog, I'll eat something up."

I go to the dope house, walk up the stairs, push the door open, and demand they give me a hit. To my surprise, they aren't bagging up dope like usual. They are loading weapons of all kinds, preparing, and planning to kill a rival drug dealer. So, from the moment I push the door open, I have ten or twelve guns pointed right at me. With my ego (having to prove myself tough) and my addiction at an all-time high, it doesn't matter to me; I just keep right on talking: "Man, give me something and I'll leave y'all alone." They are on edge and are yelling about how I could've been shot and must be crazy to bust in on them like that. They give me a few pieces to get away from them. Then they vigorously explain they don't want to see my face again and that if it had been any other night, it would've been my last.

I take my dope and go home to find the eviction notice on my door. As I get high, my reality starts to set in on me. I am certain of two things. One: I can't stay where I am; I'll run out with no place to go. Two: if I go back home to Chicago, I will be dead within a week, the way I am going for sure. I smoke all I have and then it dawns on me how very close to death I just was. I'm alone in my house with all the curtains closed, and I began speaking to God.

I explain to him how He owes me for taking up for Him when I was in the sixth grade. There was an eighth grader named Mikey, and he would go on and on about how there isn't a God, and God isn't real, and don't believe the preachers. When I heard him saying it, I told him if he said God wasn't real again, I would close his mouth for him. Mikey, being an eighth grader and much bigger, looked at me and said, "There is no God.

" I went to work on him in front of the whole school.

I said to God, "I beat him bloody defending you, God. So, if you are real, I need you to move in my life right now. You know where I am and what I need. If not, when I wake up in the morning, I'm going to quit my job, go back to Chi, and I'll be dead inside two weeks."

I make this demand on the Lord that he moves in my life and prove to me he is the one true living God while I am high off crack that I was just nearly killed for.

I fall asleep and wake up with all the same problems I had the night before. Today is Friday. I place what little valuables I have in my car. I head to work to quit, get paid, and then go back home for my final ride, I guess.

Once at work, I tell my sup, "I quit, give me my money for this week, and so long."

He says, "Well, since you're getting cash, why don't you just work today and at the end of the shift you'll have a full week's pay and go with that?"

While I'm working, the two guys come over to my station, and I'm ready to go; this is my last chance. I'm planning to cuss them to everything I can think of and fight if they don't like it. They walk over and say, "We know we give each other crap all the time, but we noticed something is different in you today; here is $400 from us both. If you need anything else, let us know." This is a lightbulb moment for me.

Then, just before lunch, my landlord calls. I answer only to tell him I can't pay him, I'm moving back home, and his keys are in the mailbox. He asks if he could come and speak with me. On my lunch break, I sit in the car with him to hear him say he wants to start over. He says to pay what I can toward the three months' rent owed and we will start with a clean slate. He will put up new carpet, new appliances, and pay me to paint my own apartment—another lightbulb moment for me. This man's attitude and demeanor toward me are absolutely different than before.

After the events with my coworkers and landlord, I realize God is revealing Himself to me. Answering my prayer in a way that I couldn't imagine in my wildest dreams. In a way, there could be no doubt it is the Lord.

When work is finished, I get in my car. It won't start—another light bulb moment. So, I catch the bus. The entire ride, I'm going over the events of the day and the night before in my head. I say to God, "OK, I know you're real now. You've flexed your muscles in a mighty way, dropped the mic on me. If I'm to stay here like you're showing me,

I need you to lay my path straight, Lord; I don't have the strength or know-how to beat my addiction."

I get off the bus at the top of a hill with a pocket full of money. I start walking down past the liquor store; nothing, I keep walking. I'm coming past a dope house, and it doesn't have one person there—on a Friday! I make it to my block and the hustlers on the corner don't even look at me. It's as if no one saw me. I get home and the key is still where I left it. Everything is there, nothing touched.

I break down and began to praise God and worship Him. The Spirit of God protected me through the gauntlet and left me with absolutely no doubt that He is real and loves me. I begin reading the Lord's word every day from a Bible my mother gave me many years ago—the King James Version. The verbiage is difficult for me to understand. At this point, three months have gone by without me having a drink, a smoke of anything, a bump, nothing, and it felt like only a weekend had passed, truly, I tell you.

One Saturday morning, before a men's meeting at the church I joined, I'm at home reading with all the blinds drawn shut, like back when I got high, and I'm getting stumped on a word. The sun keeps getting in my eye from the blinds in the kitchen—the sun is glimmering so bright through the blinds that I can't see. I go to the kitchen to adjust them, and up against the wall by the table in the corner is an NIV Study Bible. I didn't know then that this version of the Bible was even made, but God!

Now I'm a minister in training at my wife's childhood church, a senior usher, a founder of an Apostolic Church without doors, and I counsel and mentor former addicts and a soldier for Christ. All praise is due to the Lord.

Chapter Six

LET ME DO ME!

*There is a way that seemeth right,
but in the end, it leads to death.*

Proverbs 14:12

I am a thirty-year-old schoolteacher with a bachelor's and master's degree. I come from a God-fearing mother and father. I was raised in the Deep South with nine brothers and sisters in a time when Blacks were second-class citizens, at best. In the South, Blacks either made things with their hands for white folks or worked in the fields for white folks. Period, that's it. Either way, the family's livelihood revolved around and at the discretion of the abusive whites.

I'm sharing this with you so you can understand how growing up poor and suppressed in this type of system shaped some of my decisions down the road. Being a country boy, I played every sport: basketball, football, baseball, and track, every session. But basketball was my passion by far. I ran the point, and my best friend Larry played center up through our high school years, and we made a name for ourselves in our little town. Enough so that we got noticed by some scouts and were recruited. In middle school, Larry, whom I called "L, " and I made a promise to each other: at least one of us was going to the NBA. If not both, whichever one made it would bring the other along for the ride. This was a sworn oath between us two poor country kids, but then we were both recruited! Man!

We were both recruited to New Mexico State; however, they could only offer one scholarship for both of us that coming year. L was big—6'10"—so they gave him the scholarship and put me in a junior college down the way from Las Cruces. I would play for one year then join L at State when their senior guard graduated and another scholarship would open. Plus, we could play summer league ball with each other there. When I left for junior college, I had never been out of my state; it was a culture shock, to say the least. I looked different from my clothes (all hand-me-downs from my brothers) to my haircut, my talk, everything! There were guys from NYC, Chicago, Detroit, and all parts of California, and all of them had white women at the school. I had never dated or attended school with a white woman let alone spoken to one. I wanted in.

After the summer league ended and classes began for L and I, we didn't see much of each other. I hung out with my teammates and took a liking to the city boys from NYC. I liked the way they talked and dressed, their confidence, and how easy they were with white girls. It all intrigued me very much. It was an absolutely new world I didn't know was even possible. Coming from where I was, dating a white girl gave you a high probability of being killed.

One day, while in Professor Even's science class, I took out some paper to write a letter to God. I asked if He would please allow me to live however I wanted until I was thirty. I told Him, "Once I turn thirty years old, I'll give my life to you and serve you! There are so many things I want to do and experience. If you will just not take me for this sinning I plan and look forward to doing, I will stop and do right at thirty, I promise." Some nerve, right?

With this note to God, I jumped both feet in. The NY guys taught me how to steal and I got some new clothes. The Chicago teammates tuned up my speech and taught me how to rap. Then the California teammates showed me how to get the forbidden fruit I wanted so bad: white girls. Off I went, totally immersed in this greedy, lustful way of life that I now loved and longed for. In six months, my life had become more about this world than the reason I was at school: my basketball world.

In late February, three days after our last regular season game (we didn't make the playoffs), one of the white girls (who honestly a few of us, if not all of us on the team, had dated) went to the athletic director and said she was pregnant by one of the black boys on the team. The AD called the local sheriff. Now, this wasn't the South, but it was still the sixties, and the thought of these tall black boys being with this little white girl and having children didn't go over well with the school and her parents, not well at all. So, the options were jail for rape or expulsion. Just like that, I was out of school. No New Mexico State, no playing with Larry, no NBA for me. I was sent back to the country to work in the field or the factory. I couldn't tell my

Christian mother the truth about why I was kicked out of school. It would kill her (break her heart), so I said I was scared, homesick, and the work was too hard.

Once I got back to the country, I was turned out! I thought I was slick and too cool for school; you couldn't tell me nothing. I began cutting hair. I would make up crazy hairstyles and say "This is how they're wearing them in the city." While cutting hair, I met a young lady four years my senior who was a schoolteacher. She had already finished college and bought a brick house and a new Cadillac, so I thought this was my best shot at a comfortable life. After one week of knowing her and another week of dating, we got married. And before we even consummated the marriage, I was on the highway in that new Cadillac headed up to New York City to get with my partners I met in Juco (junior college). While hanging there with them, I soon picked up the drug trade, as that's how they were making a living. I loved everything about the fast pace, flash, and prestige of selling cocaine. I really felt as if I was meant to do it. Within the next four years, I'd enrolled in another school close to home in the country, married to this woman I knew nothing about for her car basically, went to the city every chance I got, and started dealing drugs. And then it happened!

My man finished school, and lo and behold, he was projected to make it to the NBA. Not only did he make it, but he got drafted as the number one pick overall. L, my best friend, had made it to the league just like we'd planned when we were small boys, but being picked as the number one draft choice was unthinkable. For the first couple of years, we went crazy. By now, my wife and I moved to a city closer to where he played and we had two small kids. I would leave them and go to the Bahamas for a month with Larry and a few women and would think absolutely nothing about it. How we set our plan was that I would have a regular job because I had a family now, but I would supply drugs to L and all his new friends in the league.

Eight years passed. I became a schoolteacher, got divorced, of course (from living like a pirate, as if I was single my entire marriage), and L's career started slowing down. But my career as a dealer was at an all-time high because of the network of NBA athletes that I supplied. I was teaching by day and dealing by night. On weekends, I would fly to Boston and Philly to unload dope. I would have work checks go bad because I didn't cash them in time.

My thirtieth birthday was a big deal. We decided to celebrate in Cabo San Lucas, Mexico. We got a private villa, and a small yacht, and everything seemed right. L, now an eight- or nine-year veteran, had wealth from the league and so did I. I had long forgotten the letter I wrote to God back in science class asking him if I could just live how I wanted until thirty, asking just to let me do whatever came to my mind and then I would serve him by giving my life over to him.

At three in the morning, I was belowdeck inside the boat in bed with two women beside me. I thought to myself, "Look at where I came from, and look at me now. I made it; this is the best life can get."

No sooner did I close my eyes then I heard a voice loud and clear as day say, "What if you died right now? You would go to hell!" I jumped out of bed, naked and shaking like a leaf. The women looked at me like I had gone crazy. This started happening to me so much over the next couple of months that I was scared to sleep. After a while, it began to happen during the day too. I kept hearing, "What if you died right now?" I really freaked out then, and I still did not think or remember anything about the letter I wrote to the Lord.

One Saturday evening, I was at home making a package to drop to a guy right across the state line. As I was walking out the door, the phone rang. It was just close enough for me to reach back within arm's length and answer before I left. The person calling was an undercover officer I knew from playing Pro-Am ball some years ago. He said "I need to speak with you right now. I'm pulling up outside your house; come get in my car." I placed the package in a safe spot in the house, came out, got in the car, and he handed me a letter.

The letter had my full name and middle initial. It stated that I am a public-school teacher as a front but that my true profession was dealing and supplying pro athletes of the NBA (top players of the time listed in order) with drugs. It had an approximation per week, my height, weight, and possible pickup and delivery points. Plus offered to make a wired purchase from me for more evidence.

After reading this letter, I got in my car, drove to the park, found a bench, and wept like a baby. I reflected on my life and all the things I had done and how this letter was the end of me. Still crying, I prayed to God, and He showed me myself in class all those years ago; the letter I wrote, how the Spirit began to convict me hours into my thirtieth birthday, the time I promised the Lord, and that both letters were connected.

I sent my guy to the stash in my house, gave him all the drugs I had, and never touched the stuff again. I went back to school, got a master's degree, and took educating seriously. I became a highly successful coach, remarried, and became a pastor of my own church. I'm still ministering at this church today as I write this testament of how I came to the Lord. Praise God!

Chapter Seven

RIGHTEOUS

To do what is right and just is more acceptable to the Lord than sacrifice.

Proverbs 21:3

I was born on a plantation in Mississippi to a single mother and two little sisters.

I was born into a system and culture of slavery, known now commonly as sharecropping.

Sharecropping is when a tenant farmer gives a part of each crop as rent and receives an agreed share of the value of the crop minus charges.

The truth of sharecropping in the south is, after slavery legally ended, this was the way the slave owners kept their slaves legally and went right on with business as usual.

There were twelve other families with us on the Avan plantation. All the houses lined up one after the other facing one another. I could look out my door and see into my father's house. He never spoke or uttered a word to me in my entire life. I only knew who he was because some of the women on the property would tell me how much I favored him. This made me furious when people would say it, because we were poor, real poor, and I would see him see us struggle. But the man never helped us with our crop duties, let alone some money, or even said hello. As if that was too much or I did something to him. Like I was his dad and had moved on with my life across the yard from him!

I was the man of the house as a kid and the only man my mother and sisters could rely on, period.

We had a hard life, but to me it was just life. Plantation duties were picking cotton: three bushels a piece per day for me and my mom, one a piece for the girls. We would go to school during the day and hit the fields in the evening. Once we planted crops and it came harvest time, they would take everyone out of school to tend the fields from sunrise to sunset, all ages, for four months. This showed me nothing was more important than money. Not school, and not health (we could be sick and we still had to tend to the crops; it would be cold and raining and we still had to tend crops). So, I got good at it and wanted to be the best. We were so good that other plantation owners would come and try to buy us from Mr. Johny, but he wouldn't sell. If you were good with the land and produced, other farmers would hear about you and then you would have a name for yourself.

Now, when harvest time came around, he would brag on us and rent us out to other farms to help them out. It felt like a good thing until I got old enough (maybe ten years old) to find out the truth. No matter how good we did in a year; no matter how many bales of cotton, bushels of peas, or ears of corn we harvested, and no matter how many trees were cleared, nothing would ever let us see a profit. Mr. Johny would say that we owed him for clothes, food, school, and living quarters for the year. We might see forty dollars for working the entire year. Forty dollars for me, my mom, and two sisters working every day except Sunday for a full year. He often said we owed him money at year's end. This changed that good feeling!

Through the years, we moved on to other plantations, thinking each one a better opportunity, until my mother got a job working inside the house for a white woman close to the city. This changed my life; I had finally made it to the great city of Memphis, and I wasn't ever going back.

I got a factory job in the city, and I was like a caterpillar shedding its skin and turning into a butterfly. The city was an entirely new world for me. New people, a new mindset, and definitely a new way of life. The guys spoke in a way I had never heard, and the women behaved in a manner altogether foreign to me. I got to the Memphis city racetrack and soaked in all that was offered.

I moved out from my mom and sisters into a place with a friend I met at a dairy farm where we both worked. After a year, his cousin moved in with us, and we became roommates and best friends. I gave a portion of my wages to my mother's household, but I was out on my own getting acquainted with the city. All three of us began working for a landscaping company. The pay wasn't that great, but we were all together, I was in the city, and it still was more money than I ever made sharecropping.

One day, we were at a factory cutting grass and bushes around the place, and an older white man came up to us while we were on break shooting the breeze.

He said, "How do you like this kind of work?"

I explained to him I liked it just fine; I got to work outside at my own pace, I got to be with my friends, and I made fifty dollars per week (which I didn't at all, but told him that since he was asking in my business).

He said, "Well, I need some help in this here factory; a few boys didn't show for work, and I'll give you two hundred dollars per week."

Inside it was for me, then! I gladly accepted his offer and worked at this company I had just been cutting grass at for fifteen years.

Having this job and making this kind of money gave me new options. I was able to help my family more, move out from my roommates into my own apartment, buy a car, and afford some indulgences, such as gambling, drinking, and fast city women. This all quickly led me to lose my apartment, wreck my car, and sleep stowed away in the factory at night without anyone knowing for two months.

Shortly after I stabilized my living, my best friend and I got another place together, just him and I. My cousin invited us to his church's revival. He had invited me personally several times before, but I hadn't gone. The day was like any other: we'd finished work, got some beer and a half pint. Then I went home to get dressed and hit up the juke joint, Catz, where we all hung out, but there wasn't much going on that night, so we thought to just swing by the revival. When I got inside, I heard the preacher speaking and became filled with the Holy Spirit. I emphatically believed that Jesus was the Son of God and knew my life would never be the same. At twenty-three years old, I was saved that very night. My best friend and I came out to the car and sat down. He looked at me in disbelief at what just happened. He took a big swig of the half pint we had been drinking on the way to church as I poured mine outside the car on the ground

He said, "I'll give you a week; you'll be right back drinking with me!"

I told him "No, I'm going to stick to it." And that's what I did.

When the Holy Spirit hit me that day, it set fire to me and consumed every facet of my life. Some months went by, and I could see the effects of God's mighty hand being on me. My best friend came home one night with his cousin and said they had a date with two sisters on the weekend and that I should come because maybe they had a cousin or a friend for me. They were living the same old way—the way I used to live. I didn't have anything in common with that anymore, especially those same type of city women who had taken me too fast a short time ago. I declined, but when they mentioned they were Mississippi girls. I thought to myself, "Maybe I should go along to check it out." In the back of my mind, I knew when I was ready to settle down it would be with a Mississippi woman, because of the values they are brought up with, and boy can they cook! City women are like snacks, but a corn-fed Mississippi woman is like a whole meal!

The weekend came and the three of us drove down to meet them. I hadn't been back to Mississippi in a long time and never planned to. The sisters were at their cousin's house (the one for me), and she was taking a little to long for my liking to come out. I was sure of who I was and who's I was. Truthfully, by the time she came out to meet me, I was uninterested. However, the girl who entertained for me the thirty minutes or so while I waited really piqued my interest, so I asked her to be my date instead of the woman who turned out to be her older sister. She reluctantly agreed after I spoke with her mother (whom I grew to love and built a very special relationship with). From that night, we dated for three months. After three months, we went out for a night of dancing. While driving her home, I advised her there was a ring in the glove compartment, and if she wanted, it was hers! She took it, and we were married that next weekend in a group wedding with my best friend, his cousin, and the sisters. (I know!). And we have been married for over fifty years.

When I got saved, I was given laser focus, confidence, assurance, and a desire to know, please, and become one with God. Not until we had our first child did, I realize the effect my relationship with my father—or lack thereof—had on me. I forgave him because God saved me, but I vowed I'd never be the type of father he was. So, I helped start a ministry. It was just a few of us, but we were mighty, with a great zeal for God. It is astounding what we witnessed the Lord do to us and through us, being of one accord. I became an evangelist, not of my idea but of request and necessity. This meant nights, evenings, and weekends out of town, out of state, or wherever the Holy Spirit took me. The only thing was, my factory worked mandatory weekends. When you're in the will of God, all things work for the betterment of your purpose. In time, all the other employees noted and took the issue to my manager that they all worked every weekend and I hadn't in over a year. He advised them in no uncertain terms that "You can't do what he does; he's doing special work." I brought all six of my children up in the Lord and he blessed me through the years to the point that my only interest became being righteous. I grew to serve God as a minister, a pastor, and then a Bishop, as I am now. I lead my own church, which allows me to touch the good Lord's people from all walks of life and teach them the principles of kingdom living.

All praise be to the Most High God.

Chapter Eight

SOMEBODY HELP ME

*The Lord is my helper; I will not be afraid.
What can mere mortals do to me?*

Hebrews 13:6

I was nineteen years old when I received salvation. My husband and I had started to go to church, and he received salvation first. He would go to a Saturday night service with his cousin and come home so enlightened and inspired to live for God. It really made me uneasy, because I hadn't made that decision yet. I just wanted to go to church and was not really ready to change my lifestyle. But my husband was committed fully to the Lord; I, on the other hand, was still smoking and was not willing to give it up.

So, one day I was in the bathroom smoking and fanning the smoke out the window so he wouldn't smell the smoke. I heard a voice in my mind saying, "You are hiding from man, but I see what you are doing." It was so real that it scared me. I dropped the cigarette in the toilet and ran in the other room, got my Bible, and began to pray. I was convinced that it was the voice of God, and I made a choice that I wanted to be saved.

The preacher began to preach that true salvation consisted of repentance, water baptism in the name of Jesus, and being filled with the Holy Ghost. I repented and got baptized, but I had not been filled with the Holy Ghost. I really wasn't seeking with my whole heart, but when our second child was born, I had an experience with the Lord that helped make up my mind without any reservation.

While I was in childbirth (the doctors would put you to sleep back then), I awoke in the middle of delivery and the pain was almost unbearable. After her birth, when I came home from the hospital, I had a dream I was falling, and fire was all around me. There was a voice that said, "You remember the pain you felt in childbirth? You got comfort knowing it would soon be over, but just think about being in that kind of pain for eternity."

It was so real that when I awoke, I was shaking. I got out of bed, went into the bathroom, and prayed, "Lord, fix me so if I should die tonight, I will be with you."

My husband's cousin (the preacher) and his wife came by our home on Christmas Eve to see the baby, and before they left that night, I asked him to pray for me and I received the Holy Ghost that very night in our living room. From that time until now, my heart has been fixed on pleasing God in every area of my life. I am fully persuaded that Jesus is my Lord and Savior, and there is nothing in this life that's more important to me than Him. That was forty-eight years ago. There have been many tests that have come in my life to challenge my faith, but by the grace of God, I have kept the faith through them all. I'm living to live again and I'm on my way to the place prepared for us by Christ Jesus. I want to inspire as many as I can to go with me.

Praise God.

I love you to life and beyond.

SHARE YOUR JOURNEY...

cortezperry@coming2christ.org

ABOUT THE AUTHOR

 Cortez Perry, an accomplished author, mentor, life coach, and marriage minister based in Milwaukee, WI, holds a Bachelor of Science in Business Management. His multifaceted roles reflect his commitment to spirituality, community, and personal development.

Affiliated with institutions like the North Side Church of God, Bible Way Outreach, and Creating Living Gems, Perry's influence spans local and international communities. Inspired by the transformative testimonies of his beloved muses, his writings blend spirituality, self-help, and biography, guiding readers on a universal journey toward faith, purpose, and salvation.

Dedicated to the memory of Pastor Steve Hibbler and Bishop Renzal Barringer, Perry's personal and professional life revolves around his faith. He treasures his family, including his wife Maria E Perry and sons Chantez

K Hines-Perry and Beckham Hudson Alphonso Perry.

Residing in Milwaukee, Perry is not just an author; he embodies his teachings, finding joy in laughter, enjoying life, and helping others. His mission is clear: inspire others to overcome challenges, discover their inner greatness, and find fulfillment in a purpose-driven life. Cortez Perry continues to be a guiding light for those seeking spiritual growth and a meaningful existence.

www.ingramcontent.com/pod-product-compliance
Lightning Source LLC
LaVergne TN
LVHW061038070526
838201LV00073B/5088